Greyfriars Bobby

Written by Michaela Morgan
Illustrated by Tony Morris

This is a story from Scotland.

It is the story of a hero who lived more than a hundred years ago.

The hero of this story is not a famous fighting soldier, or a clever inventor or a brave explorer.

The hero is a little dog – a dog called Greyfriars Bobby.

Chapter 1

Bobby was a little grey and silver dog. He was a little scrap of a dog.

He often looked a little bit ruffled and scruffy – like an old teddy bear.

He had big brown eyes, soft silky ears, strong, short legs and a very, very waggy tail.

Bobby was a happy little dog. He always looked as if he was smiling!

He spent his time with a shepherd called Old Jock. Jock was getting a bit too old to work. But he was not a rich man so he had to carry on working. Bobby helped him.

Bobby didn't really belong to Old Jock. He really belonged to a farmer and his family but Bobby did not like to sit at home in a warm farmhouse. He loved being out in the fresh air. He loved the wind in his ears. He loved the smell of outdoors in his nose – but best of all he loved Jock.

Jock was a tough old man, a man of few words. He had no family, no wife, no bairns, no house of his own. He had to work outside in all kinds of weather – even in the cold and rain. He had to sleep where he could. There was very little to make his life warm and comfortable. It was a hard life for an old man.

So Jock was not a man for soft words and fine feelings. But he had Bobby. And Bobby was a good friend.

Old Jock would talk to Bobby as if Bobby could understand. Jock would tell Bobby what a good dog he was. He would tell him what a clever dog he was. He would tell Bobby what a lively little dog he was. Jock did not actually use those words. He had his own special way of speaking.

'You're a canny wee dog, aren't you?' Jock would say, and Bobby would bark, 'Yep!' as if he agreed. 'And you're sperity too!'

'Yep! Yep!' Bobby agreed. Of course he was clever and lively! He would wag his tail so hard that his whole little body seemed to wag and he would look up to Jock with his big brown eyes full of love and loyalty.

Bobby loved to please Old Jock,
so he was quick to pick up tricks.

He could roll over and over.

He could sit up and beg.

He could lie down and stay.

He could even walk on his
back legs.

'Yes, he's a canny dog,' said Old Jock, 'and useful too.'

Yes, Bobby was a useful dog. He could catch rats. He could chase away cats and, on cold nights, he could snuggle close to his master to keep him warm.

Chapter 2

There came a time when Jock was too old to carry on his work as a shepherd. He had to leave the hills and move to live in the city of Edinburgh.

Bobby should really have stayed behind with the farmer as he belonged to him. But Bobby was not the sort of dog you could just own. He chose who was going to be his master. And he chose Old Jock.

So Bobby set off and followed Old Jock all the long and dusty way to Edinburgh.

This was about a hundred years ago. The Queen at that time was Queen Victoria. There were no cars and buses to take Jock and Bobby to the city. In the city there was no electricity. There were no radios, no televisions, no videos – but there was still plenty of noise.

Bobby was frightened by all the noise. There were so many people shouting and calling and pushing! There were so many carts rolling by! And there were so many horses' feet clip-clopping just next to Bobby's ears! It was frightening for a small dog who had just come from the peace and quiet of the hills.

15

Then in the middle of the day
there came the biggest sound of all.

BOOM!

The air shook, birds scattered,
babies cried.

'Don't you worry,' said Old Jock.
'It's the cannon – they fire it every day
at midday to let people know the time.
It lets us know it's time for dinner.'

Old Jock found a cheap eating place in the market square. He and Bobby settled down near the fire and Jock had some good broth and bread. Mr Traill, the owner, saw them.

'Out!' said Mr Traill. 'We don't want dogs in here.' But then Bobby sat up and begged. He put his paw out to shake hands and soon he was rolling over and over and walking on his back legs and performing all his tricks for the customers. Mr Traill let Bobby stay.

From that day on, Old Jock and
Bobby would wait for the boom of
the cannon. Then they would go for
their meal in the market square.
Mr Traill grew fond of Bobby. He
often saved a special bone for the
clever little dog.

Life in the town was not easy for Jock. The air was not fresh as it was in the countryside. Jock did not have a lot of money so he had to stay in the very poorest part of the town. He had to rent a cheap room and he was always afraid someone would try to steal his little bit of money and the few things he owned.

Bobby was a great comfort to him. Night after night, he kept his master warm. Day after day, he guarded his master from thieves.

With each passing day, Jock got slower and slower. He was very old now. He could not see well, he could not hear well, his legs were shaky. He was worn out and tired.

One day, Old Jock staggered back to his room feeling very ill indeed. He had been out in the cold and the rain. All night long he coughed and coughed.

During the night, when Jock was freezing cold, Bobby lay on his master's feet trying to warm them. When Jock was boiling hot, Bobby licked his master, trying to cool him down. But Bobby couldn't make Jock better.

All that night, Jock groaned and moaned. He tossed and turned and coughed and coughed and coughed. Then he sighed and whispered, 'I'm away to my home now. Goodbye, Bobby.'

Suddenly, he was very still.

Bobby understood. His master was dead. But Bobby stayed keeping watch over the body of his master. He was a faithful little dog.

For two days and nights Bobby stayed by his dead master. Finally, the police broke down the door and found the body of Old Jock. His little bit of money and his few belongings were still safe. They had been guarded by Bobby.

'Aye, that is a canny dog,' said the police. 'He's kept Old Jock's money safe. It can pay for a proper burial.'

They sent for a coffin and some men to carry Jock to Greyfriars kirkyard. Old Jock was going to be given a proper burial in a proper churchyard. He would have been pleased and proud that his life had ended in such a way.

23

Chapter 3

The men carried the coffin through
the streets. Jock had no family or
friends, no wife or bairns to follow
the coffin. But there was Bobby.

He trotted behind the coffin all the
way to the kirkyard. But just as they
were all going through the gates,
a voice bellowed, 'Can't you read?'
It was Mr Brown. He was in charge
of the kirkyard. He pointed to the
sign, NO DOGS ALLOWED.

'Oh,' said one of the men, 'let the dog in – just for the burial. He's a faithful dog looking out for his master. We'll soon be finished and then he'll be off.'

Mr Brown felt a little sorry for the dog but, 'Rules are rules!' he said. 'No dogs allowed!' And he picked Bobby up and put him outside the kirkyard gate.

NO DOGS ALLOWED

As soon as Mr Brown was not
looking, Bobby sneaked back in. He
stood by the grave and watched, as
the earth was piled on to the coffin.
Bobby stood quietly – not one 'yip' or
wag of the tail. Then he lay down on
top of the grave, as if to say, 'That's
my master in there and it's my job to
keep him company.'

The next morning, Mr Brown was surprised to see the dog again.

Bobby was lying at the foot of his master's grave, like a little furry blanket.

'Well, you're a faithful dog!' said Mr Brown. 'But rules are rules!' and he chased Bobby out of the kirkyard and slammed the gate shut. 'Now, unless you know how to open a gate, you will just have to stay out there!' he said.

Mr Brown walked back to his warm little house, leaving Bobby scratching at the gate.

Soon, people began to pass by. Bobby ran up to each one of them and scratched and whined at the gate.

Most people did not even look at the little dog. But the lads and lassies who lived all round were kinder. They patted him and played with him. Then one child opened the kirkyard gate and let Bobby in.

The next morning, Mr Brown came to check that all was well in the kirkyard. There was Bobby, lying on his master's grave.

'NO DOGS ALLOWED!' shouted Mr Brown and he ran at little Bobby. Quick as a flash, Bobby skipped out of the way. Mr Brown tried to catch him but Bobby yipped and frisked happily and slipped right out of his hands. For half an hour Mr Brown shouted and chased and Bobby trotted and tumbled all over the kirkyard.

The children heard the noise and came out to see what it was. They laughed when they saw Mr Brown trying to catch Bobby.

Mr Brown gave up, and as soon as his back was turned, Bobby lay back down on his master's grave.

Night after night, Bobby lay down on the grave. He put his nose on his paws and he stayed there all through the night.

In the end, Mr Brown gave up chasing Bobby out of the kirkyard. In fact, Mr Brown became fond of the little dog, and sometimes he even gave him a bone to chew on. The children gave him scraps too, but Bobby had a plan of his own to get food.

When the midday cannon boomed, Bobby trotted off to Old Jock's favourite eating place in the market square. There, Bobby had his dinner with Mr Traill. Then he came trotting back to lie on his master's grave.

Chapter 4

Bobby stayed in the kirkyard all through that year. He stayed through rain and wind and snow. When the springtime sun and flowers came, still he stayed. He stayed the next year too... and the next... and the next.

Every day, Bobby would wake on top of the grave in Greyfriars kirkyard. Then he'd yawn and stretch and off he'd go visiting and playing with the children.

When the cannon boomed at midday, off he would go for his dinner at Mr Traill's. Bobby made friends wherever he went. Rich people, poor people, old and young – they all stopped to smile and pat Bobby.

Everybody grew to love him. The children loved him most of all. This went on for eight years. Then one day a police officer saw the little dog lying, like a furry doormat, at the foot of his master's grave.

'Is that your dog?' he asked Mr Brown. 'Show me his licence and his collar.'

'He's not really mine,' said Mr Brown. 'He just stays here. Ask Mr Traill in the market square. The dog goes there every day for his dinner.

'Is this your dog?' the police officer asked Mr Traill.

'I wish he was my dog,' said Mr Traill. 'He's a fine dog but he just comes here to eat. Then he's off back to the kirkyard to lie on his master's grave. He's a fine, faithful dog.'

'He's a stray!' said the officer. 'And it's my job to get rid of strays.'

When the children heard about this, they were horrified.

'You can't get rid of Bobby!' they said.

'Is he your dog then?' asked the police officer.

He's nobody's dog,' said the children. 'But please let him stay!'

'If he hasn't got a collar and a licence and an owner, it's my job to take him away,' said the officer. 'He's just a stray.'

Nobody could say they owned Bobby, but many people loved him. They saw how good and brave and faithful he was, and they were ready to stand up for him.

The children started to collect every penny they could. They wanted to try to buy a licence for Bobby. It would cost a lot of money for such poor children to collect, but they found that many people in the area were willing to give a penny or two. Bit by bit, the money piled up.

Mr Traill went to the police station and begged the police officer to let Bobby stay.

'It's not for me to decide,' said the police officer. 'You will have to ask a judge about that.'

'Then I want the highest judge in all of Scotland to hear about this!' said Mr Traill. He went to the court to see the Lord Provost, the most important judge in all of Scotland.

But the Lord Provost said he could not help.

'I have to keep the law,' he said. 'The dog has no licence. He has no collar. He belongs to nobody. So, by law, he is a stray.'

As the Lord Provost was speaking, there was a loud clatter. The big doors to the court burst open and in came a crowd of poor street children, scattering pennies as they came.

'We've got some money for a licence!' they said.

The judge knew that these children were very poor.

'Have you stolen this money?' he asked them.

The children told the judge how they had all collected the pennies. Passers-by had given them pennies. Old people had given them pennies from their savings. Children had given what they could.

'Well!' said the judge. 'This is a special dog that can bring out so much goodness in people,' he said. 'But there is nothing I can do. You can't just buy a licence for any dog. You have to own it. This dog is a stray. It belongs to nobody.'

'No,' said the children. 'Bobby belongs to everybody.'

'Ah!' said the Lord Provost, 'that is the answer. The dog belongs to everybody. He belongs to the whole city of Edinburgh!'

The Lord Provost gave Bobby a collar with a medal. On the medal, it said that the dog had the freedom of the whole city. Now he belonged to all the people in the city.

43

Bobby lived on for many happy years. Every night, he lay on his master's grave. Every day, he listened for the cannon, then he trotted off for his dinner.

And all the time Bobby smiled and wagged and made friends with everyone. Even Queen Victoria became his friend.

Wherever Bobby went, he brought a smile with him. He was nobody's dog, but he was everybody's dog. He was his own dog. He became the only dog in the history of the world to be given the freedom of the city. He could go where he liked. He wasn't a stray anymore.

For fourteen long, faithful years he lived in Greyfriars kirkyard. He became famous all over Scotland and all over the world.

When he died, he was buried in Greyfriars kirkyard, near his master. A fine statue was built. It is still there. So if you are ever in Scotland, in the city of Edinburgh, you can call in and visit Greyfriars Bobby.

About the author

Michaela Morgan

I've always liked
stories about unusual
heroes and stories
about dogs – so of course I was very
keen to write the story of
Greyfriars Bobby.

The most enjoyable part of writing
for me is writing the first draft. I
gather my ideas, work out the plot
and write it in rough. After this I leave
the story alone for a while. Then I
come back to it and work on it some
more – changing, improving and
revising it.

I always read my work aloud to
make sure it sounds good. It must
sound as if I'm having a conversation
with myself!

About the illustrator

Tony Morris

I was born in Oxford and went to art school there, and later in London, at the Royal Academy. I've been painting for more than twenty years, mostly books for publishers round the world, and a film strip for BBC television called Papa Panov.

The kind of painting I enjoy most is portrait painting and I'm a member of the Royal Society of Portrait Painters. My paintings have been exhibited at many galleries in London.

I'm married and I live in the countryside of Herefordshire. I find its peace and beauty an inspiration for my work.